What Ties Us

poems by

Whitney Mackman

Finishing Line Press
Georgetown, Kentucky

What Ties Us

Copyright © 2018 by Whitney Mackman
ISBN 978-1-63534-561-2 First Edition
All rights reserved under International and Pan-American Copyright Conventions.
No part of this book may be reproduced in any manner whatsoever without written permission from the publisher, except in the case of brief quotations embodied in critical articles and reviews.

ACKNOWLEDGMENTS

"Book of Judith," *Matador Review*, Summer 2017.
"Let It Be," now titled, "Enough," *Apalachee Review*, Issue 63, 2013.
"Chippendales," *Sliver of Stone*, Issue 5, 2012.
"In Which We Make Alliances…," *Matador Review*, Summer 2017.
"Transport," *The Gambler*, July 2014.
"Isle de Jean Charles," *The Poet's Billow Literary Art Gallery*, July 2016.
"Changing Robes," *Improbable Words: an anthology of Texas and Louisiana Poets*, 2011

Publisher: Leah Maines
Editor: Christen Kincaid
Cover Art: Vinca Swanson
Inside Artwork: Lauren Boilini
Cover Design: Elizabeth Maines McCleavy

Printed in the USA on acid-free paper.
Order online: www.finishinglinepress.com
also available on amazon.com

Author inquiries and mail orders:
Finishing Line Press
P. O. Box 1626
Georgetown, Kentucky 40324
U. S. A.

Table of Contents

Private Time with Sherman Alexie 1
Leaves 3
Book of Judith 4
Enough 5
Chippendales 6
"Names Are a Consequence of Things Which Are Named" 7
How to Interpret a Woman 8
What Ties Us 9
In Which We Make Alliance among Strangers in Strange and Temporary Places 10
Transport 12
For Dr. Martin Luther King Jr. Elementary for Science and Technology 13
Isle de Jean Charles 14
Returning to Native Land 15
Space Services, Inc. 17
Changing Robes 18
On Maybe Quite Possibly Wanting to Leave New Orleans One Day 19
Finally the World Feels Poetic 20
Reckoning 22

*For my parents, Barb and Gary
thank you for teaching me to feed my happy wolf*

Private Time with Sherman Alexie
Inspired by Sherman Alexie's reading at Tulane University on October 24, 2011

I can't believe the US government
considers gay penguins
more dangerous than (part-time) Indians.
I shoot you a stare that says:
"I'd like to spend the evening with you."
See, I was an Indian too,
for five years at Cherokee Elementary.
I took our mascot seriously;
I wore a braided headband
and demanded to be called Squanto.
No need for shame before
I knew the weight of that name.

Yes, I have often battled grief,
and both of us used our teeth.
Your language washes over me.
I'm jealous you know just what to say.
Fancydancer with Verbs, I heard
you have many names, Indian names,
names you call yourself. I wonder
if you'd name me Stilted Goon
Who Stumbles Words. Regardless,
I'm almost sure we'd get along.

They think because I'm funny
that I'm less than serious.
I get that too. It's easy to ignore truth
delivered with a smile—
like what you said to Harvard:
*Yes. I'm really happy to come
speak, for free, at the college
you built on my people's bones.*
I doubt they took that seriously.

My father was a pine tree,
my mother a winter storm.
While I had a cactus
and a summer monsoon,
it seems we were raised by the same
metaphor. But, I felt this before—
when you questioned vegans
and said *gas is made of dinosaurs.*

I wish you were with me at Cherokee.
We would've made quite the crew:
curlicue Squanto Jew and stick straight Indian,
with matching feathers in our hair.
No one would mess with us—
The (Indian) Breakfast Club you always dreamed of—
if only you were there.

Leaves (after Dylan Pasture's "Mail")
"This hole in my heart is in the shape of you."
—Jeanette Winterson

This old woman, she walks out
to perfect her lawn every morning.
Crinkled leaves sprinkled over
the pruned patch: little green heaven.

She'll rake, bag what's piled, rest—
always wearing a floral shirt,
switching between the same few.

Sometimes I pass by,
look towards Leda Street,
as if I didn't know
she'd be there.
Still there, raking.

Too old to be so stubborn
in this weather. Surely
too old to be fighting
an unstoppable force.

I saw her before Hurricane Isaac.
She'd stepped up her game:
hunched over broad shoulders,
took long strokes, gathered
leaves at her feet in a hurry.

Her house wears weathered yellow
adobe, sits by St. Louis #3. I run
there by the graves most afternoons.

Once, I ran out of love
for a woman I wanted
and now I'm the one searching.

A woman, to whom I once said,
"I wonder what raking
helps her forget."

Book of Judith

I may be a widow, but I
can still seduce. Some men
will so easily believe any
lie for the taste of a woman.

Judea surrender? Yeah, right.
Distract: scent of hair, curve
of hip against picnic basket.
Come get what you deserve.

I may be a widow, but soon
hairy Holo asked me
to his tent for a late night snack—
as if I want to feed

some Assyrian asshole all
my wine and precious cheese
while Judea is surrounded,
and he gets real handsy.

Please. There was no spark between us;
he wanted my people dead.
He should have seen it coming—
my basket fit his head.

I admit it was dramatic:
his head on our ramparts.
But how else send that message?
If only there were sparks.

Enough

The horse on the balcony is becoming a problem. Come to think of it, the entire balcony is becoming a problem—with its *wanting-to-be-a-porch* attitude. I'm not even sure how the horse got there to begin with, but I know how to get it down: I need to let that balcony be a porch.

Right. Just look what happened to the trees: they pulled up by the roots and rustled away. What made this street, this oxygen, not enough? They were so well planted, so well-intentioned. That is why we have roots—so no matter how hard we sway, we stay fastened to our convictions.

I convince myself this is good for me; I tell myself *at least the horse is healthy*. But, we get on hands and knees, roll tumble bite claw hiss bite tumble roll claw hiss—much more gratifying than a make-up kiss, much more gratifying than figuring out what to do about this horse, this porch, and all the goddamned missing trees.

Chippendales

Big red barn hovers over the 5 and each time I read APPLES or CIDER—depending on the season, such different shapes for the seasons. In the blur, I feel the warmth of wood, smell the ripeness of earth, see piles and piles and piles of apples bursting to the seam, brimming to the roof, begging me to drop in from the chimney to pick my fruit as I glide down the pyramid of apples.

Last time we passed I thought I caught the name Chippendales, and in the blur I see tan chiseled beefcakes dance on top of apples, crunch apples in perfectly aligned teeth, grip apples in perfectly flexed biceps, hand apples to me because I am too busy drooling to choose, too busy sliding sexily down the pile of apples, because what isn't sexy about a pile of apples and beefcakes?

And then she says, *it's Cottondales,* and brings me from blur to the reality she located on her smart phone, and I tell her *I prefer Chippendales* as blurry beefcakes drop their apples and become puffs of cotton, without glorious pectorals, without glorious piles of apples, and when she suggests we stop for some cider, I hit the gas pedal because I can't, I just can't see reality or it will ruin my big red apple barn dream.

"Names Are a Consequence of Things Which Are Named"

Parrotfish can change gender
multiple times.

Goldfish, kept in the dark,
eventually turn gray.

Eels, oysters, worms,
guppies, frogs, and shrimp

change their sex
and sexual functions, naturally.

And yet we proceed
with such definite names.

How to Interpret a Woman

*Draw what
you see not what
it looks like*, he says
as I scribble a stick fig-
ure meant to resemble
the woman bent on
on her knees, face
on the floor,
butt in
the air.
But what I see is what it looks like, I tell him. And I couldn't
draw her or all the things she could possibly be without
excusing it as cubist,
or another skinny,
NAKED
WOMAN.
So I study
her lines,
her curves,
her moles,
while artists close one eye,
hold charcoal up to measure
her tits, thighs, waist
I write   I wonder
why we   bother be
literal w/   dimples
in skin,   buoys as
breasts   settle in.
We will   make her
how we   want her:
Skilled.   Sexual.
Smart.   Silent.
Perfect.   Perfect.

What Ties Us (after Robert Hayden's "Those Winter Sundays")

Each weekday my father got up early.
With surgeon's hands in the quiet dawn,
he buttoned his shirt and knotted his tie—
the one I picked out the night before,
in the depths of his closet, spinning both
electric tie organizers
until the perfect one came 'round.

This ritual: my kiss goodbye
since I'd never rise,
never follow "normal."
His regimen,
this regimented man,
was the balance I needed.

Yet I teased him about his beliefs
as I became a challenge
to most of them.

So, he changed the way he thinks,
but not the way he votes,
which we cannot
and will not
discuss here,
at the dinner table.

But so easily tension fades
when I remember morning back
scratches, draped over his belly
on the living room floor.

What little we knew then
of love's many and required compromises.

In Which We Make Alliances Among Strangers in Strange and Temporary Places

> *"A good story should be the perfect woman's skirt: long enough to cover the subject, short enough to keep it interesting."* —My high school English teacher

We lounge on the riverbank.
I've known you 5 days.
I tell you I don't trust people
who don't eat cheese.
You pass me the joint,
confirm your love of cheese,
and say you feel the same
about mustard. I love mustard.

We meet at the drink station.
I've known you 10 days.
I tell you I don't understand people
who don't love milk.
Tell me about it, you say,
it's a deal-breaker. Like pickles—
you have to like pickles.

We ditch fish night together.
I've known you 20 days.
You tell me you only trust people
who put filters in their joints.
I say I've done that for years.
You say that's how you knew
there's no goodbye
in an alliance like this.

We're back on the riverbank.
I've known you 25 days.
We share poems, make art.
I tell you I will miss you
and am grateful for the presence
of someone I don't know
I won't hear from again.

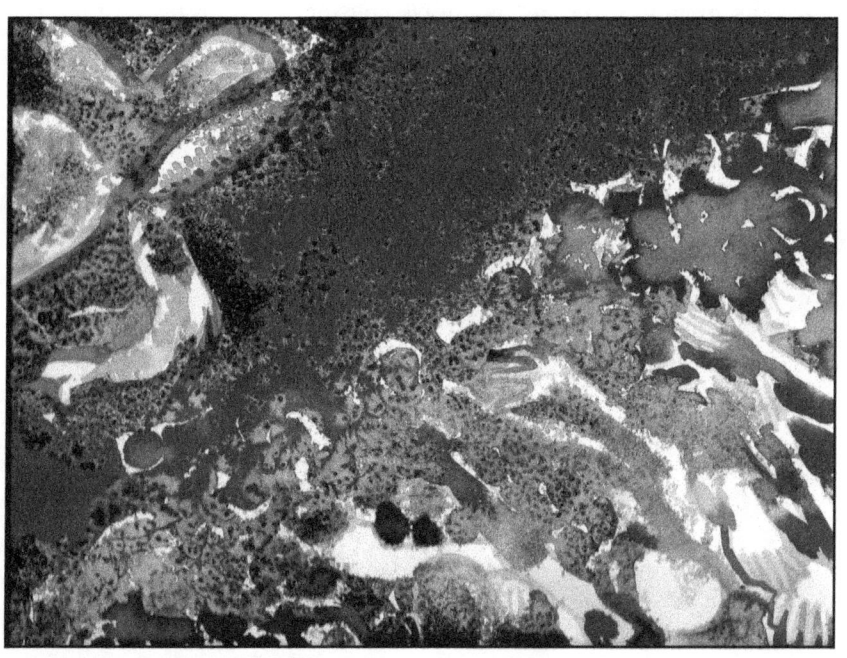

What Ties Us by Lauren Boilini

Transport

Sometimes, when I drive, I have the sudden urge to veer left and slam into the car next to me bumper-car style—but then I remember this is real life and I can't disobey traffic signs like I do when I ride my bike because taking alternative transportation puts me above the law is always chasing me cruising on my longboard wondering if they'd rather I smoke pot instead of skate this thin line between what is right around the corner and down the block I run to get away from the stress—I'm a mess before I fly because I'd like to have a fighting chance to keep myself alive I learned to stay out of the subway in the early dawn and out of cabs in unfamiliar towns I'd rather walk than trust a bus is much less nerve-wracking than being at the mercy of the waves in a little catamaran about to play bumper boats with the coast of Mexico and I'd like to teleport myself away.

For Dr. Martin Luther King Jr. Elementary for Science and Technology, March 2006

Tendons of splintered piano
baring teeth as keys grind
the mud on the sidewalk.

Spines of soggy books
smothered in soot rot
in a library reef.

Flanks of wilted doors,
hinges busted from eruption:
a classroom named "Promised Land."

Tongues of moldy ceiling tiles
flap like white flags
wilted with defeat.

Legs of desks tossed,
arms of chairs mangled,
buried with seashell binders.

Mouthfuls of lethal brown water
framed in glass block windows—
a toxic quilt in the stairwell.

In the stairwell, a huge fish!
Dehydrated, suffocated
eye socket gutted, gaping.

This is a place of learning.

Isle de Jean Charles

Too quiet: nothing
but wind whipping
through stilted bones
someone once called home.

I look over my shoulder;
I'm trespassing on sacred land.

Behind the sugar cane,
behind the levee system,
deep down in the swamps,
a quarter mile wide,
mile and a half long isle
surrenders to sink.

Too bright: squinting
to stay inside cones
on the shrinking
one-lane road.

It's only a matter of time
until the Gulf swallows it whole.

Marsh becomes bayou
becomes a new backyard.
Look away, lose an inch.
Just build it higher.
Just balance on stilts.
Just swim.

Returning to Native Land

never feels like home again
and people there treat me
as if I am the person I was
when I left. One does not
get much rest being smashed
back into an old mold.

See, I claim to have changed,
pray that I've changed,
but too often I catch myself
responding the same way.

Back and forth, I swing
this bench, in a new house
with the same silhouettes,
the same parched air—

It's so dry I can't swallow
as the 35th bug combusts
with a green flash, a sharp zap,
and the smell of burnt hair—
I accept that I'm falling in love
with you. It's not a smart thing to do,
I know this, but who am I
to get in the way of this feeling?

My friend said, *after forty,
you're not afraid to fall in love.*
I want to believe her,
but I hope I don't have to,
since I'm sitting in a perfect,
devastating landscape
and all I can think of is you.

All I can think of is you
when this is supposed to be
about the vast emptiness I feel
in this desert, under its deep purple
sky, with the Big Dipper kissing
the mountains so close
I could climb up inside.

Space Services Inc.

I laugh to think we have a star up in the sky reserved solely for us. Prime real estate built on a lie. But I gasp at "we," as in, you and me. And if I could remember the name of your anniversary gift—something gag-inducing and including secret nicknames—I'd call Space Services Incorporated and have that star reinstated to the universe

because now I'm told you're moving to town, *my town*, and I can't sit with this. In fact, I can't keep still. I'm reeling with "oh no!" and "holy shit!" and "who cares?" and "what if?" and you're affecting me, already, like you always did. And I think about "we," as in, you *and* me, and it makes me nauseous.

I already lost everything for you once, so I've kept myself from fantasies for months. But now you're here and my parents said I shouldn't dare, but you keep emailing for coffee, you keep prying back in—you under the stars of Jackson Square where you glided right towards me. And I knew it would happen, just a matter of when.

Changing Robes (after Leonard Cohen's "My Life in Robes")

After a while, you're not sure who you are.
You can't tell yourself apart from the rest.
"If it's missing it was already lost,"
a woman says, when you ask where you are.
"Or needing to relocate," you respond.
A cigarette might calm you, or kill you.
And later on, you might wish for just that—
if it's night, and tucked in lonely sheets,
or day, tricked by shadows and sounds.
Then suddenly, you remember yourself.
You know what you have misplaced:
the time.
You get dressed, because you thought you were.
You go home, because you thought you were.
You light up, because you remember why
you get married.

On Maybe Quite Possibly Wanting to Leave New Orleans One Day

I am not a very good liar,
so when you ask me if I love
the mountains more than you,
you know it's not true no matter
how many times I say: No. No baby.
Those are just boulders that speak
to my soul but you, sexy erratic
emotional pressure gasket,
are all the Mother Nature I need.
Screw the rivers and the trees.
Your peaks and valleys bring me
to my knees. Who needs
moose, bear, marmot, or deer?
I'd be happy to drown in this swamp
of beer, to ride off in the sunset
on the back of a gator. Sure, I can
go hiking, camping, biking later
when I'm old and gray and can't
light a fire for days because arthritis
flares in my fingers. I will fight
this but that doesn't mean I want to
choose. Either way I'm going to lose
because I keep telling myself I can live
without the mountains, I can live without you.

Finally the World Feels Poetic

I see smoke and trace it along the bayou,
wanting anything but home.

Firefighters shoot water in through
broken windows, water squeezes
back out through buckling wood.
Flames curl out attic corners, lick
the rooftop, taunt the firefighters.
Nothing left to burn but up up up.
The fire won't give up, and reporters
wander: *Do you live on this street?
How did it happen? How many
times did you complain about
the abandoned eyesore it became?*

Firefighters tag team, move between
hosing water, drinking water, dumping
water on heads, sitting on the curb with
water on necks in this May blaze. I feel
like I should help. Tag in. Grab the hose.
But when they use huge metal poles
with giant fish hooks at one end to rip
off the side of the house, I can't breathe.

Orange orange orange as the sidewall
disintegrates, the fire sucks in our oxygen,
the neighbor's paint melts bubbly green.

No matter what they do, the attic burns.
Finger flames still curl to the roof, still
try to climb, try to win. The soaked
wood smolders so stubbornly
the firefighters kick the front door in,
barely dodge the collapsing porch roof,
and the crowd sucks the air back in together.

I drive by the next day and the charred
skeletal frame is leveled: a demolition
machine victorious on top of the pile,
giant fist knuckles-down on the bones.

Reckoning

The sun put a gun
to his own head,
then fell splat
on my porch.

I knew if the eternal
torch could falter,
I'd better alter
my dreams.

I cleaned up
rays and debris,
took his body
to the sea,
so that Mother Earth
could rock him
as he sleeps.

The moon sensed
the doom, spying
through the clouds,
crying, the sun
got it done first.

Mountains mumbled,
rivers tumbled,
trees twisted right
off their roots.

So stars aligned
a rescue
to shoot
the world peace.

I lay down on the land
and swore to start fresh,
but I still can't seem to
burn these memories
from my flesh.

Whitney Mackman is from Arizona, but she has also called Washington, New York, Madrid, and a few tour buses home. She teaches Creative Writing at Tulane University in New Orleans and Composition at Xavier University of Louisiana. During the summer, she coaches a mountain bike team for a nonprofit in Colorado. Whitney is the creator, editor, and producer of the show CockTales™, in which men perform monologues written by other men seeking to change toxic male culture and stop sexual violence.

Whitney is lucky to be one of the last to interview Dr. Maya Angelou before she died, and the exchange is published on *The Rumpus*. That interview and some of Whitney's nonfiction can be found online at whitneymackman.com.

www.ingramcontent.com/pod-product-compliance
Lightning Source LLC
LaVergne TN
LVHW040118080426
835507LV00041B/1722